*The Moment's
Only Moment*

The Moment's Only Moment

poems

Emilie Buchwald

NODIN PRESS

Copyright © 2016 by Emilie Buchwald.

All rights reserved. Except for review purposes, no portion of this book may be reproduced in any form without the written consent of Nodin Press.

I would like to thank the editors of the following publications, in which poems in this book, sometimes in earlier versions, first appeared: *American Scholar*, "A Cabin Summer"; *Great River Review*, "Minnesota, Windchill -50°"; *Harper's*, "Winter Song"; *Kenyon Review*, "Jupiter & Io"; *The Lyric*, "Arcadia"; *Minnesota Review*, "Beauty / Beast"; *Mixed Voices*, "As Soon As It's Here It's Gone, But So What"; *Sing Heavenly Muse*, "Good-bye Good-bye"; *Sleet*, "Being Born," "Letter to Kathleen," "Yes."

Cover art: R.W. Scholes
Design: John Toren

ISBN: 978-1-935666-90-5

Library of Congress Cataloging-in-Publication Data

Names: Buchwald, Emilie, author.
Title: The moment's only moment : poems / Emilie Buchwald.
Description: Minneapolis : Nodin Press, 2016. | Includes index.
Identifiers: LCCN 2016029257 | ISBN 9781935666905
Classification: LCC PS3552.U3325 A6 2016 | DDC 811/.54--dc23
LC record available at https://lccn.loc.gov/2016029257

Nodin Press, LLC
5114 Cedar Lake Road
Minneapolis, MN
55416

*to Hank and our family,
to the memory of my parents,*

⊱

*and to the writers and readers
who keep poetry alive and lively*

Contents

1

3   Beating Time
5   Heart Throb
6   Good-bye   Good-bye
7   Flying the Hill
9   Your Eyes
11   Soul
13   From Beyond the Rainbow Bridge, Buck Comments
15   A Cabin Summer
18   My Mother's Music

2

21   Yes
23   for Barbara Esbensen, who made Thanksgiving every day
24   Poetry, the Lines Themselves
25   Suburban Mother
27   A Simple Task
29   Swimming into Sex
31   Winter Song
32   The White Book

3

35   How It Is
36   Hypocrite
36   Production Line
37   With Toast

37   Dog Soup
38   "Rats Regret Bad Choices Much As Humans Do, Study Finds"
39   Home, Home on the Range

4

43   Letter to Kathleen
47   I Will Consider Our Dog Sam
50   Possession
51   As Soon As It's Here It's Gone, But So What
53   Lipari, Aeolian Islands

5

59   Swans
61   The Imperial Gardens, Tokyo
62   Shakuhachi Flute
63   Nikko Toshogu Shrine, *O-mikuji*
65   A Bird in a Bookshop
66   Arcadia
67   You Don't Get By with Being Dead, Bill Holm
70   Tribes

6

73   The Reader
74   Jupiter/Io. These Older Nights
75   Beauty/Beast
76   Hex
77   Minnesota, Windchill -50°

7

85   Heart of Life
86   Old Dog Sleeping
87   Spring Tally
88   Games
89   At the Bird Ramada, Sonoran Desert
92   A lion and I are twined
93   Being Born
95   Cost
96   Paradise

99   Acknowledgments

1

BEATING TIME

"I dare say you never even spoke to Time!" said the Hatter.
"Perhaps not," Alice cautiously replied, "but I know I have to beat time when I learn music."
"Ah! That accounts for it," said the Hatter. "He won't stand beating. Now, if only you kept on good terms with him, he'd do almost anything you liked with the clock."
– Alice in Wonderland

Last year you drove the SUV
that glanced off mine
nudging it against the guardrail.
The meter went crazy
ringing up years
I was saving.

You advertise
the wavy ridges in my calcium-deficient nails,
the bird tracks at the corners of my eyes.

You run the video fast-forward
in realistic flesh tones.
You compress my days
into shortwave crackles
no one wants to hear.

If I could guess the rune
of your running name,
I could float a stone
or stop a clock

as I move
fast and faster
down the sloping
corridor of days,

falling
falling

spinning past those shelves,
their cakes and bottles
labeled
eat me
drink me—
gone in a blur
as I reach out a hand—

I pick up speed and know
I will not fall on leaves in wonderland.

I reach out
in the immaculate now
that is mine,
that is all I ever had,

but that has meant everything.

Heart Throb

No need to go searching for a heart of gold
since I had you, the only clock that counts,
though I never gave you much thought,
except when I felt, except when I knew,
I must surely die of grief, you, rended,
wretched, but you, no, you just wouldn't
do it, wouldn't let go, wouldn't shutter
this factory that can't take a vacation or
tolerate a strike, the Sheila E. of my one-
woman band, clipping along at 72 beats
a minute, not improvising once in the 42
million forty-eight hundred thousand
mortal moments I have consumed while
you pulsed flawlessly more than 3 billion
times, your waves washing my shores
without a break until the instant you
cease, giving me no cause to doubt,
to complain, nor one millisecond to—

Good-bye Good-bye

There we sat
at the end of our longed-for afternoon.
She was elsewhere,
and I had gone ahead,

wondering whether to take an antihistamine
with the hot dinner in the clouds,
whether there would be turbulence,
whether the lakes were finally thawed,
whether before the sun went down
there'd be a last flowering of light,
a descent into shining,

and in short and in fact,
I wasn't there.

And she was watching herself
in the black-light flicker of other eyes,
considering the best route back to the city,
what with the traffic at this hour.

We fell
through layers
of aromatic tea leaves,
drifting
by mutual consent
to the bottom of our cups.

She was elsewhere,
and I had gone ahead.

Flying the Hill

I wanted them more than anything,
ball bearing roller skates,
skates that growled.

The summer I turned ten,
my mother traded for a pair,
and, like the other girls,
I wore my skate key on a cord around my neck.

We fastened our skates
on someone's red brick stoop,
tightening the clamps with our keys
until we couldn't feel our toes.

We rolled onto the pavement,
ball bearings rumbling.
The boys in the street playing stickball
ignored us, or pretended to.

When I hit the sidewalk,
a thrum started in the soles of my feet,
vibrating every cell,
as we clattered to the big hill.

When I stepped down
to the blacktop of the street
there was silk beneath my skates,
a river made of speed.

My skates purred
as I cruised, praying
no car would turn the corner of 44th
when I flew past, eyes half-shut,
arms hugging my knees,
myself a wind,
thinking only, *faster!*

Climbing to the top
for the gift of free fall,
we surrendered
again and again
to a pleasure
we controlled,

until our bodies jittered,
our thighs burned,
legs wobbled, gave out.

Spent,
but high as the hill,
we sat in a row on the curb,
swapping candy and gum,
setting a time to fly again
before we rolled home.

Your Eyes

1

Drink to me only with them,
those palm-fringed oases.

Under your brows
they flash
danger
danger.

That black Toledo steel
thrusts to the quick.

I'm dead
before I feel the pain.

2

Snapshot
in the private booth
of your glance,

I like this one of me
Yellow ellipse / blue triangle.

I like this one of me
at Point Lobos,
riding the long night's
moony swell
rocked on its thighs.

3

Your look delivers you
unarmed
into my keeping.

It's the language
of my childhood
fully understood.

I carry it in my wallet,
alms for oblivion.

Soul

Bach
unleashed
the celestial
Sunday punch
through matter by spirit,
the hole in the bagel,
the invisible essence
without which life
would merely be
stale kaiser roll.

Wagner
forged in fire
the super loaf,
protein for superheroes,
a thick slice
for every Aryan,
easy to swallow,
heavy in the dark
eons of digesting.

Stevie,
wonder of wonders,
the blind baker,
feeds his multitude
the essentials,
love muffins,
syncopating
sweet rolls
he makes

from the honey
in his hands.

Wolfgang Amadeus,
fissioning
soul brother,
explodes
from the grave,
accelerating
at the speed
of yeast,
rises heavenward,
dissolves on my ear's tongue,
perfect
sacrament.

From Beyond the Rainbow Bridge, Buck Comments

I know you think of me sometimes,
the pup you took home, hoping
for a mellow Rin Tin Tin,
obedient, gentle, a friend to all.
But I grew and grew into
a fur mountain with suspicions,
vetoing everyone who didn't
smell like our pack.

Was it my fault I was single-hearted,
loving only the two of you and your children,
not your neighbors, who pretended to be friendly
but might have been serial killers,
not the piano tuner I cornered
behind the piano bench one afternoon,
nor those others who came once
but never again?

When strangers knocked or rang,
I waited, crouched inside the door,
but didn't give myself away with a bark.
Only a low growl betrayed my hope
you'd let in one of them,
a delivery man, a meter reader,
one of that dangerous breed in uniform
I loathed on sight.

Your children remember
my nightly rounds on silent paws,

ready to rouse and save them
from a mailman, or a pack of wolves.
When they saw my eyes
shining in the dark, they fell
into deepest sleep. I knew and they knew
that never again would they be so safe.

A Cabin Summer

1

I was afraid of the bats that swung at twilight
Out of the trees whose souls they were each day.
I was afraid to sleep alone at night
While trees slowjazzed the roof, brushdrummed my peace away.

A creek runs past, through pasture light and woods,
Over shale and crayfish, under a hutch of firs,
Spinning leaves and water striders when the year explodes
August artilleries of green, dehiscent burrs.

When I explored the creek to port, Otsego Lake,
I came upon a sloping graveljut of land
Strewn with hot puddles (languid minnows slowly baked),
And catfish eggs in pearlhoards golding in the sand.

Uneasy, like the lake spread in my singleness,
I asked, let me be alone, and I was left—alone.
I sank into the days that offered drowsiness,
And they were amber, pausing on their way to stone.

2

Ripening, as solitude is fertile for the ear,
the days prove fine and every evening fair,
I listen to discover what I hear,
Take what I discover is my share.

I watch the smoke tarnishing the clear lake gray,
Sliding the brow of hills, low on the forest's head,
Driving midges storming at the edge of day
Into the groves where sunstruck finches bed.

The air, shining with heat at noon, cools blue and thin,
While subtle lightnings sting the ground to brittle glass,
And I can see, the sun still high, the stars begin,
The day strung on the trees fall buzzing in the grass.

I wake to find my quilt and squinting pillow piled
With moon, whirling trick mirrors, smoke ropes, cloudy lures.
(No one to scold, no one to instruct the amateur—
Go back to sleep. The moon is no concern of yours.)

Hearing, too old at last for necessary lies,
Moonstruck tuskers burrow for mayapple root,
While old cabala riots in the southern sky
Gilding the meadow where she waits me out.

3

No sunset. Evening dies in haze and flood.
Hoofbeats strafe the roof. Rain flings pellets of lead.
No getaway. Flocks of leaves peck at the roaring trees,
Lilies ripple, sinking in their yellow blood

Sensing the light an ancient home,
Moths big as sunflowers decorate the pane,
Antennae seeking from the feast some crumb,
their chitin mantles staining in the bitter rain.

In their eyes the lamp finds flint and points of honey.
Spellbound, they soften, fissure, liquefy.
Spiders hunt across the window's wintry sky
For easy pickings, cockles swamped at sea.

Half-close the eyes—the world in windy spray heaves
Sidewards, listing. Perception shifts, transforming
Order, measure, color, a mutiny that leaves
Each object newly robed, ever amending.

I endlessly disown the splintered journeying,
Shipwreck where light combed like a moth's thick plume
Feathers into dark. And yet I sail and sight, willing
The voyaging between the star and compass known as home.

My Mother's Music

In the evenings of my childhood,
when I went to bed,
music washed into the cove of my room,
my door open to a slice of light.

I felt a melancholy I couldn't have named,
a longing for what I couldn't yet have said
or understood but still
knew was longing,
knew was sadness
untouched by time.

Sometimes
the music was a rippling stream
of clear water rushing
over a bed of river stones
caught in sunlight.

And many nights
I crept from bed
to watch her
swaying where she sat
overtaken by the tide,
her arms rowing the music
out of the piano.

2

Yes

These questions you ask me
with your eyes.

I would answer yes
to you always
yes   yes   yes.

I would sugar your strawberries
with my yes.

I would pack yes
into your lunches with the cookies,
crack and peel the hardest days,
and wrap them in the foil
of my shielding yes.

At night
I imagine
feeling my way
to your stabled bodies
and finding that
you have moved
out of the house,
out of the yard,
into spaces
I can't share.

I promise you
a waking passport
out of the country of casual knives

that slash because you are
too small   too tall   too blue   too red.

I promise you
something better than a promise.

You will grow
out of clothes too tight for you,
the garments of smaller persuasions.

You will grow
to imagine
yourselves.

You will grow
up   out of the leaf,
out of the shadow
of my yes.

FOR BARBARA ESBENSEN, WHO MADE THANKSGIVING EVERY DAY

Barbara, I think of you, a prism in sunlight,
loosing a rainbow from your glowing self.
You shone with the brilliance of stars, the glint of fire opal,
making words bend their wrinkled knees and dance, words
swift as the wind in cheetah's wake, playful as otter gliding in the river,
fierce as a tiger with wings.

You are the mother of books, celebrating bees, creating honey for the hive
of children discovering the golden honeycomb of words.
You built ladders to the sky, painted a water lily on the breast of night,
sang the secret lullaby of the dream mouse and his cart.

You are the grandmother whose house did not shrink but grew,
the house with room for everyone, for playing and feasting.
I think of you, a fire blazing in many colors on the hearth for those
who stretched out their hands, grateful for your warmth,
as was I, Barbara, grateful for the gift of you, whispering, "Grow!"
blessing the blades of grass that danced in the light of your joyful heart.

POETRY, THE LINES THEMSELVES

Not the words
meaning this or something
or the letters
beautiful as they are,
each a knife
to make a different cut.

Before the lights come on,
the lines rise
one after the other
in silhouette.

Meaning is blurred.
Only stance is left
and the sensation of meaning,
the room quiet
and too dark for work,
a tidal clamor in the street
dissolving.

Suburban Mother

1

A god of transport pitied me.
I'm bigger than any body now,
two ton, two tone, heavy duty,
half woman, half car,
a crossbreed of the age.

One foot idles,
dreams of naked nights
playing footsie
in sheets crisp as bacon.

One foot's the schizo,
critic and censor,
the foot with the brains,
the foot with the urge to overtake.

I hold the road in both hands,
the bowl of cherry pits,
the asphalt penance,
the nagging question
I can't remember.

Every day
I gas up and go.

2

The shortest distance between two points
is a carpool,
the lottery of children

with nothing in common
but a destination.

In the rearview mirror I watch them bob,
each in a separate wave
far from any shore.

The atmosphere is charged
with electric disturbance,
passionate wishes
that never translate into words.

3

I know my children as fellow travelers,
books and lunch bags beside them,
artists of the silent screen,
eyes blank as cut radishes.

The expensive years
we cannot ration
burn in our wake.

We left home without the list.
Our hair grows out
lead and oxides.
Our lungs fill
with lessons and errands.

Do you know us?

A Simple Task

to fetch a plate and cutlery from the cupboard and walk
across the kitchen to the stove where I was scrambling
eggs with onions and peppers, but on the way back
I disappeared into Kipling's tale of Shere Khan's death,
so cunning a tale it lit up an idea for a poem
that danced arousingly before me, and when I walked
back to the stove, it was without the plate.

By the time I had breakfast in front of me, Kipling
was gone, the glimmer of a possible poem vanished, swallowed
by the jungle from whence it sprang. Could I retrieve its spoor?
Would it return if I walked back to the cupboard? Or,
should I stand in front of the freezer, which sometimes works?

A childhood memory came winging my way.
There was my mother, saying to me, "It's a bad habit,
going off the way you do, staring into space, not speaking,
daydreaming your life away." Walking from stove to table
in a familiar flowered housedress, she was carrying
a bowl of chicken noodle soup and a bologna sandwich,
my lunch when I walked home at noon from P.S. 125.

In this command performance, my mother appeared to me
not as some template but as a real person, tender and worn,
trapped in the hostile, unfulfilling life I left behind
whenever I vanished, as I often did, into my other lives.
"Why can't you concentrate on just one thing at a time?"

she often asked, and, at that moment, I was, totally,
concentrated on her, overcome by deepest love
and sorrow, and by the simple but impossible task
of saying everything she would have wished to hear,
everything I might have said to her but never did.

Swimming into Sex

Lying at my ease,
an old Johnny Cash hit
verberating on my iPhone,
a fish called the indigo hamlet
swims into my thoughts.

Johnny sings about a ring of fire
burning burning burning
while this blue fish,
so cool cool cool,
changes gender several times a day,

do-si-do-ing without a glitch
which one will be passive,
which active,
when they switch
their fish fandango, spawn again,

as often as five times a mating.
Their stamina inspires me.
I'd like to know, as Johnny might have,
is a hamlet just as pleased
performing the role of male

as playing the female?
And is there a cutoff switch
built into their gender agenda
that tells them when to stop?
Or is the program as erratic

as the one that burns burns burns
in human DNA, urging
the consumption
of every truffle in the Godiva box
before calling it quits?

If only I could ask those hamlets
gliding without fuss
from one gender into another
whether they relish the knack, or whether
it's yet another chore in our ring of fire.

Winter Song

Cold I walk and cold I wander,
wintering the lifetime out.
Owl and weasel watch the warren
where I whimper winter doubt.
They are sure as frost and biding,
silent as the winter pause.
Naked, I can only envy
the oldest camouflage, their winter laws.

The White Book

This is your angel,
winged by your desire
to speed you on your way.

The white book is always
open to revision
to write yourself anew.

You create a new edition
with every beat
of your questing thought.

Is there darkness before you?
Send the white book
into the future

to light your way,
to light your way,
to light your way.

3

How It Is

—in honor of Ruth Stone and Carol Bly

– Mama! wails the newborn calf. Why is a man carrying me away?
Mama, I am hungry and afraid! – My darling child, every year
it is so, they take you away, though my udder is full of milk made
for you. I cry and call, but they never bring you back to me, and
I cannot follow you beyond the wire fence. The man who feeds me
says you are going to another life, and so I must be glad for you,
my darling child.

– There, there, Bossie, says the farmer, pictured on my milk carton,
embracing a cow. Never you fret. Everywhere you are revered,
prized, your natural gifts desired. You are a factory of goodness,
a vital link in the great chain of commerce that feeds the human
world. What could be better than that?

Hypocrite

    Your lifelong habit,
        eating the flesh of others,
            while you sermonize.

Production Line

    Babies in a cart,
        lambs rolling to the kill floor
            to have their throats slit.

With Toast

    Factory units
           caged in an ammonia cloud
                lay my morning eggs.

Dog Soup

    Cooked alive slowly,
            their suffering, it is said,
                makes the soup tasty.

"Rats Regret Bad Choices Much As Humans Do, Study Finds"

Imagine scientists the size of rats.
Imagine rats the size of scientists, observing scientists.
Scientists might be regretting past bad choices:

Scientist, dye in his eyes.
Scientist, back oozing from smeared carcinogens.
Scientist, electrodes in her brain to quantify terror.
Scientist, enduring shocks he can't evade
to run a maze he can't escape.
Scientist, drowning in a beaker, plucked out
to swim for her life another day.

What are the choices a scientist might not regret?

Home, Home on the Range

After roundup, we cut the calves out of the herd,
Oh, give me a home where the buffalo roam,
bawlin', callin' for ma. The mammas moo their heads off,
where the deer and the antelope play,
press against the holding pen, but they can't get out.
where seldom is heard a discouraging word
We rope the calves, slam them down, hard, so they're winded,
and the skies are not cloudy all day.
tie up three legs to make sure they can't move when
How often at night when the heavens are bright
we cut off their horns, whip off their balls, notch their ears,
with the light from the glittering stars,
burn a brand into their hides. I reckon it hurts, but heck,
have I stood there amazed and asked as I gazed,
that's the job, and, face it, they're just meat on the hoof.
if their glory exceeds that of ours.

4

Letter to Kathleen

Kathy, my friend,
how good to speak to you again.

Over the years
I've had some
faulty connections.

When I dial yesterday,
I get
busy
busy
busy
or the recording.

But you,
how have you kept that voice,
Butter Brickle Hennessy,
carbon steel vanadium,
slicing through our frozen
chunk of time?

Your voice has always
been here with me,
buried in warm sand
behind my eyes.

&

Kathy,
many beg for a message,

a whisper,
a shadow against the shade.

The milkmaid cried,
Come come oh come.
Krishna did not choose to come.

But you do not even need
to be listening
to *be* for me.

Yet, here you are.

❦

How has it been
with me?

Sometimes
I settled,
a pioneer, broken,
whose eyes
couldn't make it
over the mountains.

Sometimes I was parsley
on the platter for the ride,
a garnish uneaten.

Sometimes
I was a clear vase
filled with flowering light.

Sometimes
my bones were added to the milk
for extra calcium.

༄

Kathy,
even if you are
a wish ful-figment,

you are vine-clad,
green and primrose
primaveritas.

Your laugh floats
petal by petal, plucked
at the expense of thorns.

༄

Kathy,
even if you are
too good to be true,

true as *Lad: A Dog,*
true as milkweed pods
sailing milkweed silk,
you are true
for me.

         ❧

You are a granary
hoarded against lean years.

You are a Swiss Army knife,
many blades and all keen.

You are a stone that knows north.

You are holy.
I enshrined you.

You are a talisman.
I won't give you up.

I Will Consider Our Dog Sam

You complete our house and bless it.
Sweetness flows between us.

 ✥

Your motto: No time like the present,
where you live 24/7.

I pick up leash and collar—
you materialize.
Yes, a walk! Yes, a ride in the car!

You prance and dance,
leading the way,
tail up, a plume of energy.
Outside! Let's go!

The dog park gate clicks shut.
You spring away,
gallivant across the field,
white foam flowing on the wave.

 ✥

You are white on green,
a snowdrift on summer grass,
I on my back, you with a stick.
No conversation needed.

You are white on winter white,
white lashes, whiskers age has kinked,

invisible against the snow, except
your kohl-rimmed eyes and ruined nose.

You are the constant
force field, a presence,
in the hall,
on your rug,
beneath the desk, forepaws knuckled under,
waiting at the door.

When we come home
you scintillate
each time, a rush of joy,
smiling, thrusting your head into our hands—
Ruffle my fur, scratch my rump.
Again!

☙

You are a tender being, gentle
with the blue octopus,
red wool glove,
weathered Frisbee,
toys from puppy days,
cherished, lightly mouthed.

You are the party dog,
the family greeter, saying hello
and welcome, settling among us
for tidbits and a satisfying doze.

You stand beside us as we say good night.
You step into our photos
as if you'd conquered Hollywood,
confident that you belong in every shot
with us, your family.

Whenever there's a choice,
you choose *yes!*
You choose happiness.

꙳

Even your absence is a presence.

Out of the corner of an eye
we look for you.

You shimmer, a force field
in the hall,
on your rug,
beside the bed,
beneath the desk,
waiting at the door.

You would come to us if you could,
knowing we need you.

꙳

Your spirit is among the living.

Possession

Possession is nine points of nothing.
        A husband had me and a child
                but both names slip away.

Tell me, they say, tell me.
        But how can it be told?
They look at someone when they look in my direction.

Sometimes I see her,
        rounding a corner,
              shutting a door,
                      the one they look for when they look
                      in my direction.

Their eyes are rocks
        not cleft for me,
                the woman who screams with her teakettle,
                the potato woman boiling dry,
                      sizzling in their glance.

The light streams in,
bleaches the apron on the chair,
a crumpled cloud.

What's in those pockets?
        What's in those soft folds
                furred with dark?

As Soon As It's Here It's Gone, But So What

I remember it,
bending into the climb,
the thrust of heel and calf,
the leap of sun on rock.

Whatever it was flashed behind a bush,
lizard or snake, thin air
singing in our skulls.

A hawk hovered below us.
In his wake, birds sprawled across the sky.
Space spilled at our feet,
thin air singing in our skulls.

We were there,
immediate and true,
living in the moment's only moment.

❦

I remember it,
the room flecked with feathers of light,
snow clotting the pane,
while in the trees a soft light
splayed the spruce into fat white fingers.

The snow's thick silence
stilled the world's pulse,
and I remember the music

we made with our bones,
rising like cobras
from our twining thighs.
We were there,
bodies immediate and true,
living in the moment's only moment.

ଽ

Once I said,
I see.
I know how it is.
I know how to live in this world.
But I was wrong.
You can only know for then,
not for now.

ଽ

We keep it moving,
hand and heel and snaking thigh,
body immediate and true,

the hawk hanging
in the skull's bright air,
in the moment's only moment.

Lipari, Aeolian Islands

The motor revs.

The Zodiac bounds
forward, rubber hot under my thighs.
Sun is impartially   everywhere,
a truncheon on my flaming back,

turning the water into broth
azzurro, not blue,
opening a window down to volcanic sand
that streams away below the Zodiac's
smack smack   droning toward noon.

We fall backward
out of the swaying Zodiac
into the blood temperature of our oldest selves,
finning through transparent grottoes,
lava the volcano uttered in shudders
when the myths were made.

A cauldron of herbs simmers
between the broken fingers of the cliffs.
A mountain of pumice
pitted and quarried
has gone white blind,
staring into the glare.

The buildings waver in the heat,
centuries of sun recorded
in their thick white bones.
Built after the myths,
they have nothing to add.

The bells of Lipari
insist   insist,
tolling the end of day.
The sun flares,
a last green flicker.

Obedient sheep, one by one
the boats straggle into the harbor.
A wind blurs the water
opaque,
shutting the door into the sea.

In the midnight piazza by the pier,
I hold your hand in my lap.
We drink espresso sugared with gossip.
A fugue of blurred voices mingles
with the ground bass of the tide.

Children on the seawall run
with practiced ease, ignoring
shouted cautions, threats,
balancing in one steady hand
their cones of lemon ice,
pale as moonlight.

Out at sea
small circles of light
phosphor the water,
drift away   reappear,
fishermen seeking
honest fish by lantern light.

5

Swans

1

Black swans
sail the imperial moat
fringed by black rocks
twice as tall as a man.

The moat is dragon green,
not the element we mean
when we speak of water,
this oiled silk endpaper.

Black swans with coral beak and eye
slide on green-glaze cloisonné
under the emperor's invisible eye.

2

In summer rain,
the white swans of Kurashiki
swivel back and forth, back and forth,
under the arched concrete bridge.

Factory smokestacks spew
soap and paper, petrochemicals.
Gray plumes paint a soft, wet sky.

Warm rain rolls off the waxed whiteness
of their clipped wings.
Concealed wire netting constrains them
for the pleasure viewing of guests.

3

After dinner we stroll
in the enclosed garden of moss and rocks
at the Hotel Kokusai International.

An artificial waterfall cascades
over hollow plastic rocks.
A generator thrums,
Lights the stone lanterns at dusk.

We toss bits of dinner roll.
Carp flash, all mouth and rose-gold scales,
and we regret the bait we toss
as two swans lift themselves

almost, almost into the air
beating their clipped wings
in a thunderous yearning,
a small storm above their brackish pool.

The Imperial Gardens, Tokyo

The sign reads:
No Admittance!
Those who are drunken.
Those who bring animals with them.
Those who carry dangerous objects.
These shall become carp food!

Stifling at noon,
August sun presses
jeweled koi deep into the pond.
We are pressed. We wilt,
shaded by a captive grove
propped up on staves,
twisting to the dead gardener's will.

Long ago he beckoned them
into this dance, which we follow
along the curve of the stream.
Fulfilling their destiny,
inching toward perfection,
their wire bracelets catch the light,
cripples with shining hair.

Shakuhachi Flute

    does not spill a drop
           pouring through the stiff reed's throat
         the night heron's pond.

Nikko Toshogu Shrine, *O-mikuji*

Beneath the temple roof, the three wise monkeys,
Mizaru, Kikazaru, Iwazaru, hear no, see no, speak no evil

this cloudy autumn weekend, perched above the crowds,
below the temple roof, as a river of celebrants

circles food stalls, streams past souvenir stands
selling sets of resin monkeys, forests of paper

fortunes, tightly furled, awaiting purchase.
A woman from our tour cries out, as if in pain,

pushes others aside to reach us, thrusting
curling strips of paper into our puzzled faces.

There must be an antidote, she cries, looking wildly
at us. This, this is my husband's fortune!

*You will become incontinent, lose your soul
to a demon, your money to a scheming relative.*

We stare at one another. Nothing in our history
of fortunes in cookies has prepared us for anything

other than, *You will have a very busy year,*
or, *A lucky journey awaits you and a loved one.*

And this one, she says. How can this be mine?
This is a lie, all wrong! I've always been a good person.

Your lustful eye leads you on a crooked path.
Your children will turn away from you, wish you dead.

Our guide takes the papers from her trembling fingers,
saying, Don't be alarmed. *O-mikuji* are often wrong.

Such fortunes we send away from us. She nods at a pine
festooned with twists of paper strung on silver wires,

discarded ornaments of ill luck. On a branch she fastens,
amongst the others, these two most recent misfortunes.

Or, she asks, maybe you prefer that we burn them instead?
Once these are gone from you, you are free to choose others.

A sudden gust of rain spatters the three wise monkeys.
Hurtling toward us, the future offers its weather.

A Bird in a Bookshop

I heard the soft hooting of an owl, calling,
then a dove cooing softly, and after that,
a rill of notes, rising like a question,
soft but insistent, repeated again and again.

"That's our cockatiel," said a clerk, shelving books,
nodding at the cage that held a small bird.
"Her mate, Lancelot, died last week.
Before then, Guinevere never made a sound."

The bird watched me, the air between us alive.
She wants to know for sure, I thought.
I moved close to the cage. *I'm sorry,* I whispered,
but he's not coming back, before I fled the store.

Arcadia

In your warmth before I sleep
I hear them calling as they go,
flying the summer east and south
before the meadows fill with snow.

The vines will fall, the meadows freeze,
in spite of you, in spite of me.
The shepherd and the nymph will long
to part beneath the greenwood tree.

The green deserts the greenery.
Willows again are sticks and stakes.
Last season's vows are driven now
with leaves the changing weather takes.

The vines will fall, the meadows freeze,
in spite of you, in spite of me,
as love and idleness sink down
beneath the fabled greenwood tree.

Others will spend September nights
as freely and as well as we,
will touch and murmur in the dark
and smile at mutability.

So suddenly, so silently
the vines fall down, the meadows freeze.
To seasons and to sleep we yield
our bodies up reluctantly.

You Don't Get By with Being Dead, Bill Holm

I dreamed I saw Bill Holm last night,
alive as you and me.
Said I, But Bill, you're dead and gone.
I never died, said he.

That's truth, I said.
You never died for me.

I see you
in your Icelandic sweater,
red hair and beard gone white,
cloth book bag in hand
stocked with your newest pets.
"You must read this one," you say,
thrusting a book at me.

Insatiable, unquenchable,
your appetite for books,
stashed in every room,
on nightstands, in cupboards,
in back of the commode,
so that you and your guests might
never be lonely, might never
reach out a hand in the night
without finding a book to caress.

Music was soul food,
Bach, or a ragtime riff,
Scarlatti, Scott Joplin, Schumann,

always something new
for your fingers, feeling their way
inside the music, meditating
at the keyboard, playing Haydn
for the angel of death,
who liked it all too well.

I open one of your books.
You come striding out,
your voice with its hint
of Iceland lilt,
green Viking eyes
seeking the long view of the world,
the prairie view, horizontal grandeur,
like that other poet for whom grass
was a symbol of everything American
worth defending,
worth loving.

You hectored us, your fellow citizens:
Don't be in thrall to things!
Care about beauty, damn it!
Be less stupid!
Your love of coin will stagnate
whatever is left of your brain!

As ugly Americans, you despised us
but liked almost any one of us,
over a meal and a glass or two
of something worth drinking.

"Let's have lunch," you'd say.
"I know just the place."
You greeted the cook and the waitress
and everyone seated inside
as a friend, or soon to be one.

In an age that worships money and youth,
you said, Not so fast, America!
Look well at what poverty and age can teach.
Hard times are coming again, and you and you
and you—not a one of us will be ready.

You ate too much,
drank too much, smoked too much.
You knew the price, paid it.

You left us too soon, Bill.
We need your voice
scolding us into better.

There's unfinished business
for your words,
today and tomorrow,
as alive in times to come
as the day you scrawled them on a yellow legal pad.

Tribes

If you haven't always been one of us,
you never will be.

Don't bother to knock.
We won't let you in.

Don't stand in our sunlight.

6

The Reader

The poet floats a haiku out of her sleeve.
The reader smiles.

The poet sets off a fountain of fireworks.
The reader's sky erupts in blue and gold.

The poet suffocates a poem line by line.
The reader turns the page.

In full view of the reader, the poet saws a poem in half.
The reader closes the book, decides on a long walk.

Jupiter / Io. These Older Nights

These older nights you look more closely at your lover,
Dis: -interestedly, -passionately, -cover
the fact he's old and far too fat all over,
no more the god, and now no more the rover.

While in the bathroom mirror lurks another,
a slight resemblance to you but rather
someone not you, nor quite that scold, your mother,
a something in between, a presence still not either.

The Argus eyes that watched the gentle heifer,
the jealous eyes that made the creature suffer,
they're shut. And we are meadowed peacefully forever,
I, old cow, and you, by Jove, a duffer.

Beauty / Beast

If only she weren't such a bore!
Those large bright eyes, meaning
what? Those pearly teeth, a toothpaste ad.
The pouting mouth, the glistening lips.

She blinks doll lashes, shakes her head,
meaning—no, no, he mustn't touch.
This piety of flesh confounds him,
her silken bedroom with its iron laws.

In her fertile presence he's undone.
His fingers yearn, fumbling into paws.
He rushes to the woods to tear an animal apart,
convinced he was born fanged, without a heart.

Hex

Reject this poem.
 It will pursue you, slipping
  in silent slow motion
   through the deep snow of your sleep.
    Faster and faster you run,
     leaping   from one floe
      to another   and another
       the poem with steel claws
        not far behind.

      Reject this poem,
       this keyhole into the locked
        tower at the top of the
         labyrinth of twisting stairs
          in the house that watched you
           when you never   stepped on cracks,
            where the crow flies from the window
             shrieking   in a language
              you didn't know you understood,
               "There!   Take that one!"

           Reject this poem
            lying at your sandy feet,
             flopping and gasping
              on the shore of a cold sea
               your tears befoul,
                your heart pounding
                 as you recognize the glazed eyes
                  asking an accounting.
                   You will find it on your plate
                    tomorrow.

Minnesota, Windchill -50°
Theme and Variations

1

Mississippi
Freezes!
First of Many
Surrenders.

Tonight
something falters,

not the wind,
the black stone
fired at my chest,
the stinging nettles
in my eyes.

Tonight
something else
dies with the machinery,
the unguarded flesh.

Pity is frozen in my fingertips.

O river,
stopped in your tracks,
what can you expect from us?

Life holds on tonight
waiting for further instruction.

2

Tonight
a hot bath
and many lights for reassurance.

Tonight
the furnace guzzles fossil fuels
sucked from the last black puddles.
After this dinner,
there is no dessert.

Tonight
the wand on the roof
taps the sky
for an alternate source of energy,

canned laughter,
a torrent of light and noise
to drown out fear and tedium.
This illusion of warmth is tended
into the small hours of this night.

3

Unexplained,
those sounds outside—
a thud.
Giant fists boom against the roof

amplified   echoing
in the stone cathedral of cold.

The house suspects the worst,
brittle Rice Krispies box
settles its cardboard back to the wind.

Frost scrawls   an ugly fur
along the window ledge,
sealing us in,
sealing us off.

Lazarus himself
was not secured more carefully
the second time.

The wind hisses a curse down the flue.

4

Watch it burn,
the seasoned wood
stacked in the garage last June
by Roy the Woodman.

"This is Roy," says he in May.
"I got your oak and birch.
It's good and dry, no slugs.
Stock up while you can get it."

5

We stretch out to the music
to be warmed.

A voice pleads,
distilling pain
in purest plumped Italian,
each phrase an exquisite death.
Thank god   we don't understand the words.

A cello sobs
lamenting nature's fall from grace
into this age of lead.

Our arctic hearts dissolve.

The wind sneers.

The fire shows its orange teeth.

6

When the light quits,
cold bullies the dogs.
They lift their paws and howl
to come inside.

Rabbits are slowly freezing,
pheasants are slowly freezing
in their burrows and snow caves
without Puccini to console them.

They do not suffer the future.
Minute by minute
the present devours them.

They cannot burn
less than themselves.

7

    Tonight
    nothing is warm enough.

    Tonight
    brandy in the gullet
    won't do,
    or the down quilt,
    or a brisk quarrel.

    Tonight
    you are the live fire
    on the grate,
    you are the tale
    told to shivering children
    at winter bedtime.

You are the shield
against the black wind
roaring out of the devil's jaw.

Tonight
nothing else is warm enough.

7

Heart of Life

—for the four

When our children were young,
and we at the heart of life,
there was nothing better,
nothing more than what we had.

One winter night
that promised meteors and stars,
we woke our children,
wrapped them in blankets,
carried them outside.

Huddled at the picnic table,
we craned our necks,
staring up, rapt,
up, into a show that kept its promise,

until our eyes filled with dazzle,
until children drooped in our tired arms,
our fingers numbed,
and common sense drove us inside.

"Do you remember that night?" each child,
long grown, has asked.

We remember.

Old Dog Sleeping

Easy as snagging a treat
you do it,
stretch out fore and aft,
turn
onto your side,
sink
to the bottom
of the Marianas Trench of sleep.

If sound swims down that far,
maybe you hear
the whirr of wings rising,
the crunch of leaves
under running paws,
the flutter of the future
bringing the gift
of sleep uninterrupted.

Spring Tally

Standing ankle-deep in grass, I reckon:
The cottonwood, unkillable, survives
to hiccup cotton snow come June.
On the other hand, though cankered,
the sugar maple waves spring tassels.
Caged in chicken wire, magnolias
foiled the rabbits, opened ivory cups.
There's fresh growth in the white pines,
soft new fingers on the junipers.
The redbud, not hardy hereabouts,
is garlanded with tiny pink Dutch shoes.
Even the ancient Russian olive, loath
to show it isn't dead, has leafed.
And yet, and yet, this morning
an emerald blight is on the wing,
ash borers, a horde to suck our ash trees
dry, snuffing their shining canopies.

Steeped in a tea of aromatic greens,
awake as ever I have been,
I want to crow, a frantic rooster,
Wake up! Wake up!
Don't miss a minute!
It's a miracle to be alive.

Games

Let's say I am the first door on the right,
        and you are the convincing plot.
You are also the salt of the earth, and I am better
        than a poke in the eye with a sharp stick.
I'll be the last of a distinguished line, and you, well,
        you'll be the land time forgot.
I can be easy come, easy go. You'll be ideal
        at wanting but not wasting.

I'll play the once and only king. You'll be a spell
        Merlin sometimes forgot.
I've been the watched pot boiling over,
        while you were better late than never,
although you weren't convincing
        as the missed chance,
and I was just okay as the greener grass
        on the other side of the hill.

Tonight, we can't go wrong as the long-married couple,
you with your feet up, sports section in a heap
on the floor, savoring the last slice of homemade pie,
watching a Twins game to its bitter end,
while I linger with a book in a hot bath, because
there's no time like the present, and, for us, birds of a feather
and thick as thieves, there's no place like home.

At the Bird Ramada, Sonoran Desert

Take the sandy horse trail
that winds through barbs and spikes,
cholla, prickly pear, barrels,
desert natives
feasting   on lethal light.

Close the first horse gate after you,
turn off to the right, there, for the gravel path
hung with a carnival array of feeders.

Here's the shed, ramshackle,
open to the desert on all sides,
peeled mesquite logs
slanting inward, propping up
a wooden roof lined with ocotillo ribs.

Under that roof,
the only shade for miles,
I wait   for as long as it takes.

At a signal I can't hear,
a skittish cactus wren peers
from her saguaro penthouse, looks around,
              screams and screams again.

Birds materialize.

A flicker zooms from saguaro to feeder, back again,
and back again,

rattling out his complaint, wik-wik-wik, *scram, damn it!*
at the mob of sparrows crowding the feeder
who've heard it all before
and keep right on jam-packing in.

A troop of Gambel's quail
bursts from a mesquite thicket,
giddy as new-hatched debutantes,
head plumes   quivering, bobbing,
          peeping their delight.

A splotch of bright arterial blood
alights,   weights a slender paloverde branch,
a northern cardinal,
too red for his own good.

Plowing the air overhead,
ravens make a flyby
broadcasting the morning news,
their cries   rusty gates   opening   closing.

Higher still,
a family of redtail hunters lazes
in the updrafts,
          circling,
perusing the buffet far below.

At a signal I can't hear,
birds evaporate.

I'm alone.
No sound that I can hear.
The silence is

the desert   listening.

Flecks of mica glint from scree,
glitter from every rocky slab.

It's almost noon.

The sky is radiant
ultramarine
from one lofty horizon to the other.

Herds of pastured clouds
graze the bony shoulders
of the Rincon ridgeline.

If I could,
I'd come here every day,
for, say, a thousand years,
because this
is enough,
more than enough.

A LION AND I ARE TWINED

When she leaps   to rend
I cling
fingers taloned   in her mane.

She shakes her head and shakes me
limp but never loose.

When I stand   she goes before,
a shield of power.

If you walk behind us
I think you will be afraid,

seeing over my shoulder
those eyes   those claws
piercing my back.

Facing me,
you will observe a woman,
arms cradling a lion.

Do not judge.
The lion is not
yours   no   nor are you hers.

Being Born

Yesterday,
I watched mayflies
above a stream
making their kind anew.

Last night,
under a plankton bloom of stars
I thought about it,
my first accomplishment,
the entrance exam
given without consent.

I don't remember
twirling in warm dark,
fuzzed in fur,
greased with vernix,
sucking my thumb,
not knowing
it belonged to me
and was a thumb,

or being thrust
shuddering,
into a nova
of exploding light,
pulse after pulse
of fiery gas
propelled into
each docile cell.

I don't remember
whether stars danced,
or rain blurred the windows.
I don't remember
the hands
hefting, swaddling,
kind or impersonal.

I knew no more
than a crocus goblet,
thrusting
green and sturdy
through a March snow
the how of it or the why,
the raw insistence
on emergence.

Scooped from a cauldron
of gene soup,
I beat the odds,
became
a universe.

Cost

The cost is what it is,
built into the frenzy
of each spindling cell.

If we could pause in time,
if I could keep your glance,
which is more to me than history,

I'd have you out of nature if I could,
out of this milkweed chronicle,
if any coin were good.

The cost is what it is.

I hold you,
a mountain stream
playing through my life's cupped hands.

Paradise

We were waiting for a train in the echoing underground.
I was thirteen. He was old, a family friend, a refugee from another century.
The Gestapo hammered at his front door with the order for his arrest
as he walked out the back door with nothing but his passport in his pocket.
Just before our train thundered into the station, making it impossible to hear,
out of the blue, he said to me, memory is a paradise no one can expel you from.
This morning, in another century, I woke up, remembering.

Acknowledgments

Almost fifty years ago, in 1967, Norton Stillman became Minnesota's literary publishing pioneer as publisher of Nodin Press; a few years later, in 1972, he opened the independent bookstore Micawber's, where small press titles were welcomed. Remarkably, time has not diminished his enthusiastic advocacy for poets and writers. I thank him for the pleasure of publishing this book with Nodin Press.

Heartfelt thanks to R. W. Scholes for creating the stunning art on the cover of this book, one of his beautiful, unique pastels.

I am grateful to Deborah Keenan, poet and teacher of poets, for her insights. I asked Deborah to read the final manuscript of this book; she was enthusiastic, but she was also able to see, as at that point I could not, what I might want to jettison or rearrange. Her students are fortunate indeed.

My thanks to John Toren, Nodin Press's book designer, for his skill, his exacting standards, and his patience.

My gratitude to Laurie Buss Herrmann for her consummate copyediting and proofreading.

I would like to thank each of the poets whose work I had the honor of editing—and learning from—at *Milkweed Chronicle* and Milkweed Editions.

I would also like to acknowledge how much I have benefitted from living most of my life in a mecca for writers and readers, a place where great libraries, writers' organizations, a variety of bookstores, and a bounty of literary publishing flourish.

This book was set in Galliard, a font created
by Matthew Carter based on the work of
sixteenth-century French type designer
Robert Granjon.